— THE GOURMET KITCHEN —
GARLIC

WRITTEN BY ORLA BRODERICK
ILLUSTRATED BY JANE STROTHER

SUNSET PUBLISHING CORPORATION
MENLO PARK, CALIFORNIA

A QUARTO BOOK

Library of Congress Catalog Card Number: 93-087761

ISBN 0-376-02756-8

This book was designed and produced by
Quarto Publishing Inc.
The Old Brewery, 6 Blundell Street
London N7 9BH

Editors: Kate Kirby, Laura Washburn, Susan Ward
Art Editor: Mark Stevens
Designer: Julie Francis
Art Director: Moira Clinch
Editorial Director: Sophie Collins

First published in North America in 1994 by Sunset Publishing Corporation
Menlo Park, CA 94025

First printing May 1994

Typeset in Great Britain by Central Southern Typesetters, Eastbourne, UK
Manufactured in Hong Kong by Regent Publishing Services Ltd.
Printed in China by Leefung-Asco Printers Ltd.

Contents

INTRODUCTION

CULTIVATION & VARIETIES

Cooking with garlic — lots of garlic — has become fashionable. Either the worries of social acceptability have been abandoned, or the offense itself is suppressed by chewing parsley, cardamom seeds, or dry toast. One reason for garlic's acceptance is its healthy reputation. In ancient times, Virgil declared garlic "essential to maintain the strength of the harvesters," and on the great pyramid at Giza is an inscription about the garlic eaten for extra strength and good health by the men who built it.

Growing Garlic

Garlic is a member of the large *Allium* genus, to which chives, onions, shallots, and leeks also belong. The best conditions for growing garlic are a sunny location, organically enriched and well-drained soil, and consistent moisture. To grow, first break a head of garlic into individual cloves; then bury cloves (broad, blunt end down) about 1 inch deep and 4 inches apart. In mild winter climates, plant garlic in

4

autumn for early summer harvest; in areas with cold winters, plant garlic in early spring for harvest in late summer.

When leaves start to yellow, cease watering and bend foliage to the ground to hasten maturity. Dig bulbs when leaves have yellowed completely, remove as much soil as you can, then let bulbs dry — but not dry out — under cover, then store in a cool, frost-free place. Fresh garlic is sweet, mild, tender, and plump, with skin that clings closely.

With time, the skin becomes papery, the bulb more wrinkled and yellowed, and the flavor sharper. This is the garlic that is

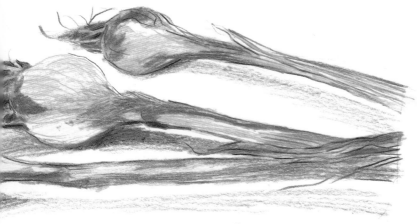

most readily available. Although the individual cloves are still juicy, enough moisture has evaporated from the outer layers of skin to keep the garlic firm for months. When choosing store-bought garlic, look for bulbs that are closely packed together and firm when squeezed.

Eventually a green, slightly acrid-tasting shoot starts to grow from the center, and hard or moldy patches may even appear on the outside. If the age of garlic is suspect, cut the cloves in half and remove any signs of the green bud. Stubborn skins can easily be removed by placing the cloves in boiling water for 15–20 seconds.

Types of Garlic

The three most common types of culinary garlic are white-, pink-, and violet-skinned: white-skinned garlic, such as that grown in California, is the mildest, but it only lasts 4–6 months; pink-skinned "rose" cloves are of medium strength and keeping quality; and violet-skinned garlic, generally considered superior, is supposed to have the strongest flavor of all, and it may keep for a year or more. Elephant garlic is actually an ancient ancestor of the leek and not a true garlic. Its large size seems to be its biggest asset; it often has a bitter aftertaste and is best avoided.

Another member of the *Allium* genus is garlic chives, otherwise known as Chinese chives or *ku chai*. The leaves are usually sold in Chinese and Oriental markets. They can be used in the same way as ordinary chives — bearing in mind that their flavor is stronger and has a hint of garlic — and are also good stir-fried or braised as a vegetable side dish.

COOKING WITH GARLIC

A chicken roasted with 40 garlic cloves has a much more subtle garlic flavor than a salad tossed with just one or two crushed raw cloves. Though this may seem unlikely, it is true. Proper cooking (burned garlic can be very nasty indeed) transforms the strong, pungent taste of raw garlic into a mellow, buttery tang. In some recipes garlic can actually be more of a main ingredient than an incidental flavoring.

Used as a seasoning, garlic gives greater depth of flavor, highlights other flavors, and produces wonderful background tastes. The more the structure of a clove is broken down, the more flavoring oils will be released. So, if garlic is finely chopped before cooking, its flavor will be pungent; if left whole, it will simply add a delicate hint. (When sautéing, for example, heat a whole peeled clove in the butter or oil and remove it from the pan when there is a waft of garlic aroma.)

Raw garlic should be used with discretion. Garlic is rich in a unique sulphur containing a flavorless amino acid called alliin. However, as soon as garlic is crushed, alliin converts to allicin, which gives off its characteristic powerful smell and taste. Add raw garlic to a dish promptly,

8

and do not let it sit around too long, as stale garlic is unpleasant, both in flavor and aroma!

Other ways to introduce garlic's flavor include adding a clove or two to bottled oil to be used in cooking and salad dressings, or to the water when poaching eggs or boiling potatoes. (*Note* Oils flavored with garlic either must be refrigerated or have an acid such as vinegar added to them in order to prevent botulism.) You can also insert cloves into potatoes when roasting or baking, or infuse them in milk or cream before making a white sauce or a dish like Gratin Dauphinois (see page 52). Try placing a few peeled cloves under the skin when roasting or braising poultry or into the flesh when roasting meats. When ready, mash the garlic with the cooking juices to make a sauce.

Preparing Garlic

If using many cloves of raw garlic for a recipe, split the head of garlic with a solid punch of the fist. Otherwise detach a single clove from the bulb. Peel away the papery skin, cut in half lengthwise and, if necessary, remove the green growing shoot in the center, which can give a bitter taste. Then finely chop, slice, or cut into slivers, as the dish requires.

To crush garlic, place the flat of a heavy knife blade over the clove, with the handle outside the edge of the cutting board.

Use the heel of your palm and strike the flat blade sharply to slightly crush the clove and loosen the skin, which can now be easily peeled. Then use the tip of a round-bladed knife and a good pinch of salt to mash the clove, working from the tip to the root end. Continue the process of mashing and mixing until smooth. (This can be done on a piece of wax paper to avoid having to scrub the board later.) Steer clear of "the lethal garlic press," as described by Elizabeth David, the well-known English food writer, because it may impart a crude metallic and acrid taste to the garlic and, hence, the finished dish.

A slightly acrid taste may also be noticed in commercial garlic salt and purée, which are no substitutes for the real thing. Happily, both can be made at home: the first simply by adding a couple of unpeeled cloves to the salt jar; the second by simmering whole, unpeeled cloves in water for about 40 minutes, or until softened. Drain well, skin, and purée with salt and a dash of olive oil. Store in a glass jar in the refrigerator (freezing will compromise the flavor).

GARLIC & HEALTH

People have cherished garlic as a folkloric cure as far back as history can take us. Even now, it is used as a medicinal plant throughout the world. A regular diet of garlic — considered most effective when raw — is thought to be helpful for a variety of ailments. Extensive scientific research attempts to show that garlic is a diverse and potent remedy. Some modern medical research (about ¼–⅓ of all studies) shows what the ancient

Egyptians suspected and generations of Chinese and Europeans believed — garlic may indeed be a power to be reckoned with.

The effects of garlic fall into two broad categories. The first is a natural antibiotic, antiseptic, and antifungal agent. Garlic juice in the laboratory has been shown to be almost as powerful as penicillin. It may be possible to make use of garlic's antibacterial properties at home. There are folk remedies that use garlic for running noses, bronchitis, sinus problems, indigestion, constipation, and mild stomach upsets. If you suffer from cystitis or other urinary infections, there are popular garlic remedies for those, too.

But by far the most exciting development is garlic's suspected ability to protect and improve circulation. Researchers hope to prove that it can lower blood cholesterol, reduce the body's own production of fats, and prevent blood clotting. In countries where large quantities of garlic are eaten, the death rate from heart attacks is lower. However, more studies are needed to prove all of these claims.

Garlic-Yogurt Cheese with Crudités

2 cups plain yogurt

1 large clove garlic, crushed or minced

3 tablespoons chopped mixed fresh herbs, such as chives, parsley, dill,

oregano, basil, or tarragon

2 teaspoons honey

1 teaspoon salt and small pinch freshly ground black pepper

1 pound mixed crudités, such as broccoli flowerets, baby carrots, radishes,

cherry tomatoes, and celery stalks

Combine the yogurt, garlic, herbs, honey, and seasoning in a bowl. Place a double layer of cheesecloth in a strainer and spoon in the mixture. Place the strainer over the bowl and allow to drain for 4 hours. Chill overnight.

Serve the cheese accompanied by the crudités. *Serves 4–6.*

Garlic Toast with Olive Paste & Tomatoes

8 slices ciabatta bread or Italian
    country bread, sliced 1 inch
    thick and lightly toasted on
    both sides
1 large clove garlic, halved
2 teaspoons capers

40 pitted black olives
¾ cup extra-virgin olive oil
8–10 fresh basil leaves
Pinch each salt and freshly ground
    black pepper
4 ripe tomatoes, coarsely chopped

*R*ub the toast slices all over with the garlic and reserve the garlic. Arrange the slices side by side on a large platter. Place the garlic in a food processor along with the capers, olives, ⅔ cup of the oil, most of the basil, and the salt and pepper. Blend until just combined.

Spread the olive paste over the toast slices and distribute the tomatoes on top. Drizzle with the remaining oil, if desired. Tear the remaining basil leaves and use to garnish the garlic toast. Serve at room temperature. *Serves 4.*

Roasted Garlic with Herbs

4 firm heads garlic

⅔ cup chicken or vegetable broth

⅓ cup olive oil

2 thyme sprigs

2 rosemary sprigs

1 teaspoon coarse sea salt

1 loaf French bread

*P*reheat the oven to 350°F. Trim the papery skin off the top of the garlic to just expose the tips of the cloves. Arrange in a small ovenproof dish, and pour the broth around them. Drizzle 1 tablespoon of the oil over each garlic head, tuck the herbs around them, sprinkle with the salt, and bake for 1 hour, basting every 15 minutes, or until the cloves are tender and golden. To serve, squeeze the cloves out of their skins, spread onto warm or toasted French bread, and drizzle over any juices. *Serves 4.*

Eggplant Pizzas

1 large eggplant
⅓ cup olive oil
3 cloves garlic, crushed or minced
1 small onion, sliced
14-ounce can tomatoes, chopped, or 1 pound fresh tomatoes, peeled,
seeded and chopped
1 tablespoon coarsely chopped fresh oregano
⅓ teaspoon salt and small pinch freshly ground black pepper
½ cup each shredded mozzarella and Cheddar cheese
4 oregano sprigs
Few basil leaves, chopped

Preheat the oven to 350°F. Cut the eggplant into thick slices and brush all over with half the olive oil. Place the slices in a single layer in an oiled ovenproof dish. Smear the tops with half the garlic, cover loosely with foil, and bake for 40 minutes.

Meanwhile, heat the remaining oil and gently cook the onion and remaining garlic until softened. Add the tomatoes and oregano. Cook for 10 minutes more, then add the seasoning. Remove the dish from the oven, spread each slice of eggplant with the tomato sauce, sprinkle with the cheese, and return to the oven for 5–10 minutes, or until the cheese bubbles. Garnish with oregano and basil and serve at once. *Serves 4.*

Mushroom Fila Tartlets

5 ounces fila pastry, thawed if
    frozen
½ cup butter, melted
1 clove garlic, minced
2 shallots, minced

1 pound mixed mushrooms, sliced
½ cup dry white wine
1 teaspoon fresh thyme leaves
Large pinch each salt and freshly
    ground pepper

Preheat the oven to 400°F and lightly grease four 4-inch tart pans. Cut the pastry into twelve 4-inch squares, brush them with half the butter, and use them to line the tart pans, rotating each pan a one-third turn for each layer to create a jagged edge. Bake for 10 minutes until golden.

Meanwhile, over medium heat, sauté the garlic and shallots in the remaining butter until just golden. Add the mushrooms, wine, and thyme. Sauté for 2–3 minutes, add the seasoning, then spoon into fila tart shells. *Serves 4.*

Fennel-roasted Peppers

4 large red bell peppers
2 small fennel bulbs
3 cloves garlic, sliced
⅓ cup extra-virgin olive oil
Large pinch salt and small pinch freshly ground black pepper
3 tablespoons finely chopped fresh flat-leaved parsley

*P*reheat the oven to 350°F. Cut the bell peppers in half lengthwise, and remove the seeds. Arrange in a lightly oiled, shallow ovenproof dish, cut side up. Slice the fennel bulbs lengthwise into eighths, keeping the layers attached to the root ends. Blanch in salted water over high heat for 5 minutes. Drain and set aside to cool.

Arrange two slices of fennel in each pepper half. Scatter over the garlic, drizzle with oil, add the seasoning, and bake for about 1 hour, or until tender. Transfer to a serving dish, spoon over the juices, and sprinkle with the parsley. Serve warm or at room temperature with plenty of bread to mop up the juices. *Serves 4.*

Garlic & Sorrel Soup

2 tablespoons butter

6 cloves garlic, crushed or minced

5 cups chicken or vegetable broth

½ cup finely shredded sorrel

Large pinch salt and small pinch
    freshly ground black pepper

⅓ cup semolina pasta

2 eggs, beaten

⅔ cup whipping cream

2 tablespoons garlic croûtons

Melt the butter and gently sauté the garlic over medium heat for 1 minute. Add the broth, sorrel, and seasoning. Bring to a boil over high heat, then gradually stir in the semolina. Reduce the heat, cook gently for 10 minutes, then remove from the heat and, beating all the time, add the eggs and cream. Stir well, ladle into warmed bowls, and garnish with the croûtons. *Serves 4.*

SALADS

Mixed Vegetable Salad

Egg-safe Hollandaise
1 tablespoon tarragon vinegar
⅓ cup water
2 egg yolks
½ cup plus 2 tablespoons unsalted
butter
1 clove garlic, crushed or minced
3 tablespoons chopped fresh
tarragon

Large pinch salt and small pinch
freshly ground black pepper

1 pound baby new potatoes, halved
1–1½ cups each baby vegetables,
such as carrots, cauliflower
flowerets, corn, and sugar snap
peas, blanched

To make the hollandaise, boil the vinegar and water over high heat until reduced to 1 tablespoon. Remove from heat, cool slightly, then slowly beat in the yolks. In a separate pan, heat the butter, garlic, and tarragon to 220°F (use a quick-read thermometer). Place the egg mixture over a bowl of 150°F water and whisk in the hot butter mixture in a steady stream. Continue for 3 minutes until thickened. Season and set aside.

Cook the potatoes in boiling salted water for 8–10 minutes. Drain. Arrange the vegetables on a platter and spoon over the hollandaise. *Serves 6.*

Egg-safe Caesar Salad

1 egg white
1 tablespoon lemon juice
5 tablespoons extra-virgin olive oil
2 cloves garlic, crushed
1 tablespoon whole grain mustard
1 teaspoon each superfine sugar and
    Worcestershire sauce
Large pinch salt and small pinch
    freshly ground black pepper

2 slices day-old white bread, crusts
    removed and cut into ½-inch
    cubes
¼ cup freshly grated Parmesan
    cheese
1 romaine lettuce
2-ounce can anchovy fillets,
    drained and chopped

To make the dressing, mix the egg white with the lemon juice, place in an airtight container, and chill for at least 48 hours but no longer than 4 days (upon longer standing, the egg begins to solidify). Just before serving, place the egg mixture in a food processor or blender, add 4 tablespoons oil, half the garlic, the mustard, sugar, Worcestershire sauce, and seasoning, and process until blended. Preheat the oven to 400°F. Toss the bread cubes in 1 tablespoon oil with the remaining garlic and half the Parmesan. Spread on a baking sheet and bake for 10 minutes until golden. Tear the lettuce and place in a salad bowl. Pour the dressing over, and toss to coat. Sprinkle with the croûtons, the remaining Parmesan, and the anchovies. *Serves 4.*

Roasted Tomato Salad

6 beefsteak tomatoes

¼ teaspoon salt and large pinch
   freshly ground black pepper

2 large cloves garlic, minced

12 pitted black olives

24 small fresh basil leaves

3 tablespoons extra-virgin olive oil

2 tablespoons Parmesan cheese
   shavings

*P*reheat the oven to 400°F. Plunge the tomatoes into boiling water for 1 minute, remove, and drain. Peel off the skins, halve the tomatoes crosswise, and arrange in an ovenproof dish, cut side up. Season with the salt and pepper and sprinkle with the garlic. Place an olive and a couple of basil leaves on each one. Drizzle with olive oil and bake for 1 hour. Top with the Parmesan shavings; serve warm or at room temperature. *Serves 4.*

Broiled Pepper Salad

2 each red and yellow bell peppers, quartered lengthwise and seeded

Small pinch each salt and freshly ground black pepper

⅓ cup extra-virgin olive oil

2 teaspoons balsamic vinegar

1 clove garlic, crushed or minced

5 pieces sun-dried tomato in oil, cut into strips

3 tablespoons torn fresh basil leaves

*B*roil the peppers, skin side up, until they are thoroughly blackened and blistered. Drop into a plastic bag, tie a knot in the top, and set aside until cool enough to handle. Remove the skins and cut the peppers into strips.

Arrange the pepper strips on a platter with any juices. Season with the salt and pepper. Drizzle with the oil and vinegar, add the garlic and sun-dried tomatoes, and gently turn the vegetable strips to coat. Sprinkle with the basil and serve at room temperature. *Serves 4–6.*

Warm Beef Salad Niçoise

1 pound baby new potatoes	1½ cups green beans, trimmed
4 beef fillet steaks, each 2 inches thick	12 anchovy-stuffed green olives
2 large cloves garlic, halved	1 small Bermuda or red onion, halved and sliced
¼ pound cherry tomatoes	¼ cup olive oil
¼ teaspoon each salt and freshly ground black pepper	3 tablespoons red wine vinegar
	2 tablespoons Dijon mustard

Cook the potatoes in boiling salted water for 10 minutes, or until tender. Drain. Rub the beef all over with one of the garlic cloves, discard the garlic, and broil the steaks on a rack for 5 minutes, turning once. Season the tomatoes with half the salt and pepper, add to the rack with the meat, and broil for 2 minutes more. Set aside to rest. Blanch the beans in boiling water for 2 minutes, rinse, and drain.

Place the potatoes, tomatoes, and beans in a salad bowl; add the olives and onion. Slice the beef thinly and add to the salad. Crush the remaining garlic and place in a screw-top jar with the oil, vinegar, mustard, and the remaining salt and pepper. Shake until combined. Drizzle over the salad and serve. *Serves 4.*

Baby Potato & Lima Salad

1 pound shelled lima beans, fresh or
   frozen

1 pound baby new potatoes

2 mint sprigs

Dressing

½ cup olive oil

3 tablespoons lemon juice

½ teaspoon lemon zest

3 tablespoons snipped fresh chives

1 teaspoon superfine sugar

Large pinch salt and small pinch
   freshly ground black pepper

*I*f using fresh lima beans, blanch them in boiling salted water over high heat for 1 minute. Drain, rinse under cold running water, slip the beans out of their skins. Return the beans to the pan. Cook the blanched (or frozen) beans for 5 minutes, or until tender. Drain. Cook the potatoes with the mint sprigs over high heat in boiling salted water for 15–20 minutes until tender.

Meanwhile, make the dressing. Beat the oil, lemon juice and zest, chives, sugar, and seasoning until well combined. When the potatoes are cooked, drain them, and transfer to a serving bowl. Add the beans and the dressing while the potatoes are still hot and toss thoroughly to coat. Serve warm or cold. *Serves 4–6.*

Chèvre Salad

1 clove garlic, sliced

Large pinch salt and pinch freshly
  ground black pepper

4 tablespoons walnut oil

1 tablespoon raspberry vinegar

1 teaspoon snipped fresh chives

¾ pound mixed salad leaves

4 slices chèvre (goat's cheese)

1 red-skinned pear, cored and sliced

½ cup walnuts, toasted and chopped

*P*reheat the oven to 300°F. Place the garlic and seasoning in a salad bowl. Mash to a paste with the back of a spoon. Add the oil, vinegar, and chives. Beat until blended, then add the salad leaves and toss to coat. Place the chèvre on a lightly oiled baking sheet on the top shelf of the oven and warm until it just begins to melt, then arrange on the salad with the pear slices. Sprinkle with the walnuts and serve. *Serves 4.*

27

VEGETARIAN DISHES

Spicy Couscous

1/4 cup olive oil
4 small cloves garlic, slivered
2/3 cup couscous
2 1/2 cups vegetable broth
1 tablespoon soy sauce
3 tablespoons mild curry paste

1/4 cup mango chutney
1/2 cup golden raisins
1/3 cup snipped fresh chives
4-inch piece cucumber, seeded and
    chopped
2 red apples, cored and chopped

*H*eat the oil in a casserole over medium heat and sauté the garlic until lightly golden. Add the couscous and cook gently for 2 minutes; set aside.

In a saucepan, mix together the broth, soy sauce, curry paste, chutney, and golden raisins. Bring to a boil over high heat. Stir the curry mixture into the couscous, mix well, and remove from the heat. Cover the casserole tightly and leave for 20 minutes. Remove the lid, stir in the chives, the cucumber, and the apples. Serve warm or cold. *Serves 4.*

Pesto, Tomato & Zucchini Flan

¼ cup fresh basil leaves, plus a few sprigs for garnish

2 cloves garlic

½ cup pine nuts

3 tablespoons olive oil

5 tablespoons freshly grated Parmesan cheese

Large pinch each salt and freshly ground black pepper

1 sheet (about 8 ounces) frozen puff pastry dough, thawed

1 teaspoon milk

3 small Roma or plum tomatoes, thinly sliced

1 zucchini, thinly sliced

Preheat the oven to 400°F. For the pesto, place the ¼ cup basil leaves, garlic, and pine nuts in a food processor and blend until fairly smooth. Add all but 2 teaspoons of the oil, the Parmesan, and half the pepper. Blend well.

Roll out the pastry dough on a floured board to a 10-inch circle, place on a greased baking sheet, and prick all over. Brush the edges with milk and spread the pesto almost to the edge.

Arrange the tomatoes and zucchini on top of the pesto in overlapping layers. Brush with the remaining oil and season with the remaining salt and pepper. Bake 25–30 minutes until the pastry has risen and is golden brown. Serve warm, garnished with the basil sprigs. *Serves 4.*

Roasted Winter Vegetables with Garlic Paste

16 cloves garlic, tips sliced off

8 small carrots

4 turnips, quartered

4 small parsnips, halved

8 small red-skinned potatoes, quartered

1 small winter squash, peeled and cubed

Few sprigs each fresh thyme and rosemary

¼ teaspoon each salt and freshly ground black pepper

½ cup olive oil

1 baguette French bread

Preheat the oven to 400°F. Place the garlic, all the vegetables, and most of the herbs in a large roasting pan, sprinkle with the seasoning, drizzle with the oil, and toss to coat in the oil. Cover and bake for 45 minutes. Remove the cover, turn the vegetables, and return them to the oven for another 30 minutes, or until the vegetables are tender and golden. Transfer the vegetables to a serving dish. Pick out the garlic cloves, remove and discard the skins, and mash garlic to a paste with the pan juices. Spread the paste over the vegetables, garnish with the remaining herbs, and serve with the bread. *Serves 4–6.*

Herby Potato Pie

1 sheet (about 8 ounces) frozen puff pastry dough, thawed
2 pounds salad potatoes, thinly sliced
¼ teaspoon each salt and freshly ground black pepper
3 cloves garlic, minced
⅓ cup chopped fresh mixed herbs, such as parsley, oregano, and thyme
⅔ cup whipping cream
1 egg, beaten

Preheat the oven to 375°F. Roll out three-quarters of the pastry dough large enough to line a 2½-pint dish; then layer the potatoes in it, sprinkling each layer with a little of the salt, pepper, garlic, and herbs. Pour the cream and most of the egg on top. Roll out the remaining pastry dough and use to cover the pie. Brush the top with the remaining egg. Bake for 1 hour, or until golden. Serve warm or cold. *Serves 4–6.*

Green Risotto

6 cups vegetable broth

6 tablespoons butter

2 cloves garlic, minced

2 shallots, minced

1½ cups arborio rice

½ pound mixed green vegetables,
   such as peas, sugar snap peas,
   small broccoli flowerets, and
   green beans

½ cup freshly grated Parmesan
   cheese

⅓ cup chopped fresh parsley

¼ teaspoon salt and large pinch
   freshly ground black pepper

Bring the broth to a boil over high heat, then reduce heat and keep at barely simmering point. Meanwhile, in a large, heavy-based saucepan, melt 2 tablespoons of the butter, add the garlic and shallots, and sauté gently for 5 minutes, until soft but not colored.

Add the rice to the pan. Stir until well coated in butter. Add 1 cup of broth and cook over low heat, stirring frequently, until the broth is absorbed. Add the remaining broth one cup at a time. When three-quarters of the broth has been added, stir in the vegetables. Continue cooking and adding broth until the rice is tender and all the broth has been absorbed. Stir in the remaining butter, the Parmesan, and the parsley. Season with the salt and pepper and serve hot. *Serves 4.*

Gorgonzola Pizza

1½ cups self-rising flour
1 teaspoon baking powder
½ teaspoon salt
1 tablespoon chopped fresh oregano
12 pitted black olives, thinly sliced
5 tablespoons olive oil

3 tablespoons water
4 cloves garlic, minced
½–¾ pound Gorgonzola cheese, cubed
Small pinch freshly ground black pepper

Sift the flour, baking powder, and salt into a bowl. Stir in 2 teaspoons of the oregano and the olives. Make a well in the center, add 3 tablespoons of the olive oil and the water; mix to a soft dough. Roll out to fit a 9-inch ovenproof skillet.

Heat 1 tablespoon of the remaining oil in the pan. Gently cook the dough over medium-low heat for 4–5 minutes, until the base is golden. Turn out onto a baking sheet, add the remaining 1 tablespoon of oil to the skillet, then slide the dough back in, uncooked side down. Cook for another 4–5 minutes. Sprinkle the garlic and cheese over the dough.

Cook until the bottom of the pizza is golden, then broil until bubbling. Garnish with the remaining oregano and the pepper. *Serves 4.*

33

Ricotta & Spinach Gnocchi

1⅓ cups ricotta

1 pound frozen spinach, thawed, drained, and finely chopped (or 2 pounds fresh spinach, cooked, drained, and chopped)

2 eggs, beaten, plus 2 yolks

1½ cups all-purpose flour, plus extra for dusting

1½ cloves garlic, crushed

½ cup freshly grated Parmesan cheese

¼ teaspoon each salt and freshly ground black pepper

⅔ cup whipping cream

Handful fresh sage leaves

Sauce

1½ cloves garlic, crushed

½ cup freshly grated Parmesan cheese

½ cup sun-dried tomatoes, preserved in oil and drained

1 teaspoon fresh sage leaves

⅓ cup olive oil

1 teaspoon lemon juice

Small pinch each salt and freshly ground black pepper

*B*eat together the ricotta, spinach, beaten eggs, flour, garlic, Parmesan, and the seasoning. With the help of a hot, wet teaspoon, shape the dough into oval dumplings about the size of a small walnut. Dust your hands with flour and roll each dumpling lightly in flour. Place on a baking sheet and chill for 1 hour.

Meanwhile, to make the sauce, place all the ingredients in a food processor. Blend until smooth.

To cook the gnocchi, place in boiling salted water over high heat and poach for about 10 minutes, or until they rise to the surface of the water. Remove with a slotted spoon, drain, and cool. Arrange the gnocchi in an ovenproof dish.

Beat the egg yolks with the cream, pour over the gnocchi, and turn to coat. Place under the broiler for at least 5 minutes, or until golden. Transfer the gnocchi to warmed plates. Top each serving with a generous dollop of the sauce. Garnish with the sage leaves and serve at once. *Serves 4.*

MEAT & POULTRY

Chorizo & Cherry Tomatoes

¾ pound chorizo, or other spicy sausage, thickly sliced

6–8 ounces thick-cut smoked Canadian bacon, cut into matchsticks

1 Bermuda or red onion, halved and sliced

2 cloves garlic, crushed or minced

1 pound mixed red and yellow cherry tomatoes

½ cup pitted black olives

Small pinch salt and large pinch freshly ground black pepper

⅓ cup chopped fresh parsley

Sauté the sausage and bacon over medium-high heat for 2–3 minutes, until browned. Remove and drain on paper towels. In the fat left in the pan, sauté the onion and garlic until lightly colored, about 6 minutes. Add the tomatoes and olives and cook for 3–4 minutes more, until the tomatoes are just warm. Return the meat to the pan, season with the salt and pepper, sprinkle with parsley, and serve at once. *Serves 4.*

Red-hot Ribs

Sauce

2 teaspoons chili oil

4 large cloves garlic, crushed or
    minced

3–4 small fresh chiles, seeded and
    finely chopped

2/3 cup tomato catsup or paste

2/3 cup malt vinegar

5 tablespoons honey

2 tablespoons Dijon mustard

Large dash Worcestershire sauce

1 1/3 cups chicken broth

Large pinch each salt and freshly
    ground black pepper

4 pounds lean pork spareribs

Preheat the oven to 375°F. To make the sauce, heat the oil in
a saucepan over medium heat. Add the garlic and fresh chiles,
and stir-fry for about 30 seconds. Add tomato catsup or paste,
vinegar, honey, mustard, Worcestershire sauce, broth, and
seasoning. Bring to a boil over high heat and simmer gently for
10 minutes.

Arrange the ribs in a large roasting pan. Brush with a little of
the sauce. Roast for 30 minutes, then drain off any fat. Spoon
the remaining sauce over the ribs and roast for 1 hour more,
turning and basting occasionally. *Serves 4.*

Bacon & Walnut Pasta

1 pound fresh penne

½ cup shelled walnuts, finely
    chopped

Sauce

1 tablespoon vegetable oil

½ pound lean bacon, cut into thin
    strips

4 small cloves garlic

⅓ cup soft cream cheese

⅔ cup half-and-half

2 teaspoons chopped fresh thyme
    leaves

Small pinch salt and large pinch
    freshly ground black pepper

*B*ring a large pan of salted water to a boil, and cook the penne, stirring once, until just tender. Meanwhile, make the sauce. Heat the oil in a skillet, add the bacon and garlic, sauté for about 5 minutes, or until the bacon is browned and crisp. Discard the garlic. Lower the heat and add the cheese, mashing until it just begins to melt. Pour in the half-and-half,

add the thyme and seasoning, and heat gently, stirring until thickened.

Drain the pasta, return it to the pan, and toss with the sauce and the walnuts. *Serves 4.*

Mini Meatball Pita Pockets

¾ pound lean ground lamb
1 clove garlic, crushed
1 teaspoon ground cumin
1 egg yolk, beaten
¼ teaspoon each salt and freshly
   ground black pepper
4 pita breads
2 carrots, coarsely grated
4 tomatoes, halved, seeded, and
   diced

Tzatziki Sauce
1 cucumber, peeled
1 clove garlic, crushed
½ cup plain yogurt
3 tablespoons chopped fresh mint
Pinch each salt and freshly ground
   black pepper

Mix the lamb with the garlic, the cumin, egg yolk, and seasoning. Shape into small meatballs, and broil for 5 minutes, turning once, until cooked through. Transfer to a plate and keep warm.

To make the *tzatziki,* coarsely grate the cucumber and squeeze out as much water as possible, using your hands. Then mix it with the garlic, yogurt, mint, and seasoning. Cover and chill.

Broil the pita for about 30 seconds on each side, then cut in half. Gently ease open each half and fill each pocket with meatballs, carrots, and tomatoes. Drizzle with the *tzatziki* and serve. *Serves 4.*

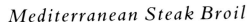

Mediterranean Steak Broil

4 sirloin steaks, each 1-inch thick and trimmed of excess fat

⅔ cup olive oil

2 large cloves garlic, crushed or minced

3 tablespoons sun-dried tomato paste

⅔ cup red wine

3 tablespoons torn fresh oregano

¼ teaspoon each salt and freshly ground black pepper

1 small eggplant, cut into 2-inch thick slices

1 red bell pepper, halved, seeded, and cut into eighths

2 small zucchini, cut in half lengthwise

¼ pound small yellow pattypan squash

8 asparagus tips

1 rustic crusty loaf

Place the steaks in a shallow non-metallic dish. Mix together ⅓ cup olive oil, the garlic, sun-dried tomato paste, red wine, oregano, and the seasoning. Pour over the steaks and turn to coat. Cover and marinate for at least 1 hour in a cool place or up to 24 hours in the refrigerator.

Add the eggplant, pepper, zucchini, squash, and asparagus to the marinade with the steak. Turn to coat, cover, and marinate for another 30 minutes in a cool place.

Remove the steaks, eggplant, pepper, zucchini, squash, and asparagus from the marinade and arrange on the broiler rack. Broil for about 10 minutes, or until cooked as desired, basting with the remaining oil and turning occasionally. Pour the marinade into a small pan and heat gently until reduced a little. Arrange the steaks and vegetables on serving plates and drizzle some of the reduced marinade over each. Serve with the bread for mopping up the juices. *Serves 4.*

Herbed Hamburgers with Guacamole

4 pounds chuck or sirloin steak,
   trimmed and coarsely chopped
2 cloves garlic
1 tablespoon Dijon mustard
Handful fresh cilantro leaves
¼ teaspoon each salt and freshly
   ground black pepper
1 large onion, cut into ¼-inch rings
⅔ cup milk
6 tablespoons flour, seasoned with
   ⅛ teaspoon each salt and freshly
   ground black pepper

Oil, for deep frying

Guacamole

1 ripe avocado
1 small clove garlic, crushed or
   minced
1 tablespoon lime juice
1 tomato, peeled, seeded, and
   chopped
½ teaspoon chili powder
¼ teaspoon each salt and freshly
   ground black pepper

Place the steak, garlic, mustard, cilantro, and seasoning in a food processor. Blend until just combined; do not over-process or the meat's texture will be too heavy. Shape the meat into eight patties. Set aside.

Cut the onion into ¼-inch slices, separate into rings, place in a bowl, and pour the milk over. Cover and set aside until needed.

To make the guacamole, cut the avocado in half, and scoop out the flesh. Mash the flesh with a fork, add the garlic, lime juice, tomato, chili powder, and seasoning. Mix well.

Cook the hamburgers under a hot broiler for about 2 minutes on each side, or until done to your liking. Meanwhile, toss the onion rings, a few at a time, into the seasoned flour; then deep-fry until golden. Drain on paper towels. Place two hamburgers on each plate, top with generous dollops of guacamole, and scatter the onion rings on top. *Serves 4.*

Butterflied Leg of Lamb with Rustic Potatoes

1 4-pound leg of lamb, boned and butterflied

1 small head garlic, each clove cut into slivers

4–5 fresh rosemary sprigs

½ cup olive oil

1 tablespoon lemon juice

2 pounds potatoes

¼ teaspoon each salt and freshly ground black pepper

Spread out the butterflied lamb on a clean work surface. With a sharp pointed knife, make a small cut every inch or so into the skin of the meat. Push one of the garlic slivers and

2–3 rosemary needles into each incision. Reserve the unused garlic slivers and rosemary sprigs. Place the meat in a large non-metallic dish. Mix 2 tablespoons of the olive oil with the lemon juice, and brush over the lamb. Cover, and marinate for at least 2 hours, or overnight in the refrigerator.

Transfer the lamb to a broiler pan. Position no more than 2 inches away from the heat, and broil on high for 15 minutes on each side, or until the lamb is cooked as you prefer. Remove from the broiler and allow the meat to rest, covered, for 5–10 minutes before carving across the grain into thick slices.

Meanwhile, peel the potatoes and pat dry. Cut into 1-inch cubes and season with the salt and pepper. Heat the remaining olive oil in a large skillet over medium heat. Add the potatoes and remaining rosemary sprigs. Cook for 15 minutes, tossing occasionally. Stir in the remaining garlic, cook for 5 minutes more, and serve with the leg of lamb. *Serves 4–6.*

Chicken Livers with Chile Pasta

1 pound fresh tagliatelle

1 serrano chile

⅓ cup olive oil

2 cloves garlic, sliced

½ pound chicken livers, trimmed
   and cut into strips

4 scallions, chopped

Large pinch each salt and freshly
   ground black pepper

3 tablespoons torn fresh cilantro
   leaves

Cook the pasta in a pan of boiling salted water until tender to bite. Drain.

Meanwhile, seed the chile and slice thinly. Heat the oil over medium heat and sauté the garlic and chile for about 1 minute, until they just begin to brown. Add the chicken livers and sauté for 2–3 minutes. Then add the scallions and sauté for 1 minute more. Pour the chicken liver mixture over the pasta and mix well. Season with the salt and pepper, sprinkle with the cilantro leaves, and serve.

Serves 4.

Duck Braised with Garlic

1 duck (about 4 pounds)

42 cloves garlic

2 sprigs each rosemary, sage, and
thyme

2 celery stalks, sliced

¼ teaspoon each salt and freshly
ground black pepper

2 pounds potatoes, cut into pieces

4 leeks, thinly sliced

4 tablespoons butter

⅓–½ cup sour cream

2 tablespoons chopped fresh parsley

Preheat the oven to 375°F. Cut off any excess neck skin from the duck. Pull out the fat from inside the body cavity. Cut along one side of the breast bone to the neck cavity and then cut along both sides of the backbone. Halve the duck and remove the bone. Cut each half into two pieces.

Place the duck pieces in an ovenproof casserole. Add all but 2 of the garlic cloves, the herbs, celery, and half the seasoning. Cover with a tight-fitting lid and bake for 1½ hours.

Meanwhile, cook the potatoes in boiling salted water for 15–20 minutes, or until tender. Drain and set aside. Crush the 2 remaining garlic cloves and sweat with the leeks in the butter over medium-low heat until softened. Mash the potatoes with the leek mixture, sour cream, and remaining seasoning. Remove the duck from the casserole, garnish with the parsley, and serve with the mashed potatoes. *Serves 4.*

Honey & Mustard Turkey

4 half turkey breasts (about 6 ounces each), skinned and boned

3 tablespoons olive oil

2 cloves garlic, crushed

1 tablespoon honey

1 tablespoon whole grain mustard

3 tablespoons torn fresh basil leaves

3 tablespoons tomato paste

¼ teaspoon each salt and freshly ground black pepper

Cut each turkey breast horizontally three-quarters of the way through. Open out, and place the butterflied breasts between two pieces of wax paper. Pound with a meat mallet to a ¼-inch thickness. Combine the oil, garlic, honey, mustard, basil, tomato paste, and seasoning. Spread over the turkey breasts. Place the breasts on lightly oiled foil under a hot broiler and cook for 4 minutes on each side, basting occasionally with pan juices. *Serves 4.*

Spicy Chicken Kebabs

3/4 cup whole blanched almonds

12 chicken thighs, skinned, boned,
    and cut into pieces

1 cup plain yogurt

4 cloves garlic, crushed

1-inch piece fresh ginger, peeled
    and crushed

Juice of 1 lime

1 teaspoon ground coriander

1/2 teaspoon ground cumin

Large pinch ground turmeric

1/2 teaspoon each salt and freshly
    ground black pepper

3 cups cooked rice

1/2 cup mango chutney

1 lime, cut into four wedges

Spread the almonds on a sheet of foil, then bake in a hot (400°F) oven for about 5 minutes, or until toasted. Cool and finely chop. Place the chicken in a shallow non-metallic dish. Mix the almonds with the yogurt, garlic, ginger, lime juice, coriander, cumin, turmeric, and the seasoning. Pour the mixture over the chicken and turn to coat the pieces. Cover and marinate for at least 30 minutes or up to six hours.

Meanwhile, soak eight bamboo skewers in cold water for 30 minutes. Pat dry, then thread the marinated chicken pieces onto the skewers. Broil on high for 10–12 minutes, turning once. Serve at once with the rice, chutney, and lime wedges. *Serves 4–6.*

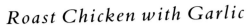

Roast Chicken with Garlic

1 chicken (about 4 pounds), rinsed and wiped dry
8–10 garlic cloves, peeled
4 tablespoons butter
¼ teaspoon each salt and freshly ground black pepper
6 bacon strips
1¼ cups chicken broth
⅔ cup dry white wine
1 tablespoon fresh tarragon leaves

Preheat the oven to 350°F. Season the chicken cavity with some of the salt and pepper, and insert the garlic cloves. Rub the chicken all over with the butter and remaining seasoning. Cover the chicken breasts with the bacon strips and place in a large roasting pan. Pour the broth and white wine over the chicken.

Roast for 2–2½ hours, basting with broth every 15 minutes, until the meat near the thigh bone is no longer pink. Remove the bacon to allow the breast to brown and sprinkle the chicken with tarragon leaves. Cook for 15 minutes more.

Transfer the chicken to a serving dish. To make the gravy, pour off as much of the fat as possible. Stir the remaining juices thoroughly, until all the sediment is scraped from the pan and the gravy is rich brown. Place the roasting pan directly on the burner and boil for 2–3 minutes over high heat to reduce. Serve the chicken hot, accompanied by the gravy and the roasted garlic. *Serves 4–6.*

Crunchy Tomato-coated Chicken with Gratin Dauphinois

Gratin

2 pounds salad potatoes, peeled and
   thinly sliced

2½ cups half-and-half

⅔ cup milk

2 cloves garlic, crushed or minced

1 cup shredded Gruyère cheese

¼ teaspoon each salt and freshly
   ground black pepper

½ cup olive oil

16 sun-dried tomatoes, finely
   chopped

4 cloves garlic, crushed or minced

⅓ cup chopped fresh parsley

2 teaspoons fresh thyme leaves

¾ cup dry bread crumbs

1 chicken (about 4 pounds), cut up

½ teaspoon each salt and freshly
   ground black pepper

2 eggs, beaten

Preheat the oven to 350°F. To make the *gratin,* put the potatoes, half-and-half, milk, and garlic in a saucepan. Bring to a boil over high heat. Reduce the heat and cook gently for 10 minutes, stirring constantly.

Using a slotted spoon, remove the potatoes from the pan, and layer them in a buttered, shallow ovenproof dish, alternating with one-third of the cheese and seasoning. Repeat twice more, pouring the creamy cooking liquid over the potatoes on the top layer and ending with the remaining cheese and seasoning. Bake the potatoes for about 1 hour, or until tender and brown.

Meanwhile, put the oil in a roasting pan and place it in the oven. Mix together the tomatoes, garlic, herbs, and bread crumbs. Season the chicken pieces with the salt and pepper, dip into the beaten eggs, and coat evenly in the bread crumb mixture. Remove the preheated pan from the oven, add the chicken pieces, and baste well. Bake for 40 minutes, turning once. Then pour off the excess oil and bake for 5 minutes more. Serve the chicken pieces with the *gratin. Serves 4–6.*

Crispy Garlic Chicken

2 eggs
4 cloves garlic, crushed or minced
1/2 teaspoon each salt and freshly
    ground black pepper
4 chicken breast halves, skinned
    and boned
4–6 cups baby new potatoes
4 cups baby carrots

4 tablespoons butter
1/2 cup fresh white bread crumbs
1/4 cup freshly grated Parmesan
    cheese
3 tablespoons chopped fresh parsley
3 tablespoons vegetable oil
2 tablespoons minced fresh parsley

*B*eat the eggs, garlic, and half the seasoning to blend, then pour over the chicken in a shallow dish. Chill for at least 30 minutes or up to 2 hours. Meanwhile, steam the potatoes and carrots for 15 minutes, or until tender crisp. Remove from heat. Melt 2 tablespoons of the butter and keep warm.

Mix together the bread crumbs, Parmesan cheese, parsley, and remaining seasoning. Coat the chicken with the mixture. Heat the remaining butter and the oil in a heavy-bottomed skillet, and fry the chicken over medium heat for 7–8 minutes on each side, or until the juices run clear. Toss the vegetables with the butter and parsley. *Serves 4.*

54

FISH & SEAFOOD

Spiced Coconut Mussels

4 pounds fresh mussels

4 tablespoons butter

2 shallots, minced

2 cloves garlic, minced

1-inch piece fresh ginger, peeled
    and crushed

1 stalk lemongrass, finely chopped

14-ounce can coconut cream

1¼ cups dry white wine

3 tablespoons chopped fresh
    cilantro

¼ teaspoon each salt and freshly
    ground black pepper

Few cilantro sprigs

Clean the mussels thoroughly under cold running water; pull off the beard with a quick tug, scrub if needed, and rinse. Discard any that remain open.

Melt the butter in a large heavy-bottomed saucepan, add the shallots, and sauté gently over medium heat until softened. Add the garlic, ginger, and lemongrass. Sauté for 1 minute more. Stir in the coconut cream, wine, cilantro, and seasoning.

Bring to a boil over high heat, then add the mussels, cover, and shake well. Cook for about 5 minutes, shaking the pan frequently, until all the mussels open. Discard any that remain closed. Pile the mussels into bowls, divide the cooking liquid among them, and garnish with cilantro. *Serves 4.*

Stuffed Baked Sea Bass

1 whole sea bass (about 3 pounds), cleaned and scaled, with head left on,
if desired
2 cloves garlic, minced
2 shallots, minced
⅓ cup chopped toasted almonds
1 tablespoon each chopped fresh parsley and tarragon
⅔ cup dry white wine
Grated zest and juice of 1 lemon
1 tablespoon melted butter
¼ teaspoon each salt and freshly ground black pepper

Preheat the oven to 400°F. Rinse the fish and pat it dry, then place the fish on a large piece of buttered foil.

Mix together the garlic, shallots, almonds, and herbs. Stuff the cavity of the fish with the mixture. Drizzle the wine and lemon juice over the fish, then brush with the melted butter. Sprinkle the lemon zest and seasoning on top. Seal the edges of the foil well, to keep in the juices.

Place the foil packet on a baking sheet. Bake for 30 minutes. If serving the sea bass hot, leave in the foil for 15 minutes before serving. If eating cold, remove the skin while still warm. *Serves 4.*

Tuna with Lime & Green Herb Sauce

⅓ cup olive oil

4 cloves garlic, sliced

1 medium onion, chopped

4 tuna steaks, about 6 ounces each

¼ teaspoon each salt and freshly
    ground black pepper

6 sprigs each cilantro, parsley,
    and basil, coarsely chopped

3 tablespoons capers

Grated zest and juice of 1 lime

2 pounds baby new potatoes,
    steamed

Heat the oil in a skillet over medium-high heat. Sauté the garlic and onion for 3–4 minutes, until just softened. Remove from the pan. Season the tuna steaks and sauté them for 3–4 minutes on each side, or until just cooked as desired. Return the garlic and onion to the pan, then add the herbs, capers, lime zest and juice, and cook for a few minutes more. Serve at once with the potatoes. *Serves 4.*

Jumbo Shrimp Sautéed in Garlic

4 tablespoons butter

2 tablespoons vegetable oil

4 cloves garlic, crushed

24 jumbo shrimp, shells intact

6 tablespoons brandy

¼ teaspoon each salt and freshly ground black pepper

1 lemon, quartered

*I*n a large, heavy-bottomed skillet, stir the butter and oil over medium heat until the butter is melted. Add the garlic and sauté quickly for 10 seconds, then add the shrimp and continue to cook over high heat for 5–6 minutes, shaking the pan constantly. Add the brandy and seasoning. Serve at once with the lemon wedges. *Serves 4.*

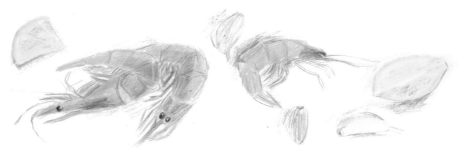

Monkfish with Tomato & Pepper Sauce

3 tablespoons olive oil

2 cloves garlic, minced

1 Bermuda or red onion, halved and
    sliced

1 each red and yellow bell pepper,
    seeded and sliced

¾ cup sliced mushrooms

2 small zucchini, sliced

1¾ cup fresh tomatoes, seeded and
    chopped

4 tablespoons torn fresh basil
    leaves

1 bay leaf

4 pounds monkfish fillets, skinned,
    boned, and cubed

½ teaspoon each salt and freshly
    ground black pepper

8–12 pitted black olives

3 cups cooked brown basmati rice

*H*eat the oil in a large heavy-bottomed saucepan and gently sauté the garlic and onion over medium heat until softened. Add the peppers, mushrooms, and zucchini, and continue cooking for about 5 minutes, stirring constantly. Add the tomatoes, 3 tablespoons of the basil, and the bay leaf. Cover, reduce the heat, and simmer gently for about 10 minutes. Then uncover, raise the heat, and allow the sauce to reduce a little. Discard the bay leaf.

Add the monkfish and the seasoning. Cook for 5 minutes, until the fish is just cooked through. Garnish with the olives and remaining basil. Serve at once with the rice. *Serves 4.*

Steamed Trout Fillets with Stir-fried Snow Peas

4 rainbow trout fillets (about 6 ounces each)
4 thin slices fresh ginger, peeled and finely shredded
6 scallions, finely shredded
1 tablespoon soy sauce
1 tablespoon rice wine or dry sherry
1 tablespoon sesame oil
2 cloves garlic, thinly sliced

Stir-fried snow peas
3 tablespoons vegetable oil
1 clove garlic, crushed or minced
1 pound snow peas, trimmed
2 teaspoons soy sauce
1 tablespoon toasted sesame seeds
¼ teaspoon freshly ground black pepper

Place the trout fillets on a large heatproof plate. Sprinkle with half the ginger and scallions. Fill a steamer or large saucepan with 3 inches hot water and bring to a simmer. Place the fish on the rack of a steamer or on a rack set into the pan, and cover tightly. Steam gently for about 15 minutes, or until just cooked through.

Remove the rack from the steamer. Lift off, and discard the ginger and scallion mixture. Drain away any liquid that has accumulated around the trout. Sprinkle the remaining scallions, soy sauce, and rice wine over the fish.

Pour the oil into a small saucepan. Over medium heat, gently sauté the remaining ginger and the sliced garlic, until just golden brown. Pour the mixture in a thin stream all over the trout and keep warm.

Meanwhile, heat the vegetable oil in a wok over medium-high heat, then add the garlic. Cook for 10 seconds. Stir in the snow peas, and cook, stirring, for 3–4 minutes. Add the soy sauce, sesame seeds, and seasoning, and toss to coat. Serve the snow peas at once with the trout.

Serves 4.

Bouillabaisse

Aïoli
1 egg white
2 tablespoons lemon juice
2 cloves garlic, crushed
2 tablespoons water
2 teaspoons Dijon mustard
1 cup olive oil

Large pinch saffron threads, mixed
*   with 3 tablespoons water*
⅓ cup olive oil
4 cloves garlic, crushed or minced
2 pounds mixed firm-flesh white
*   fish fillets, such as monkfish, sea*
*   bass, or snapper, cut into*
*   2-inch pieces, trimmings reserved*

2 onions, finely chopped
2 leeks, finely chopped
5 cups water
Few sprigs parsley, thyme, and
*   1 bay leaf, tied in a bundle*
½ pound tomatoes, peeled, seeded,
*   and chopped*
Grated zest of 1 large orange
½ teaspoon whole fennel seeds
¼ cup chopped fresh parsley
½ teaspoon each salt and freshly
*   ground black pepper*
4 medium potatoes (about 2
*   pounds), cut into chunks, boiled,*
*   and kept warm*

To make the aïoli, combine the egg white and lemon juice. Place in an airtight container and chill for at least 48 hours, or up to 4 days (upon longer standing, egg begins to solidify). Place in a food processor or blender with the garlic, water, and mustard and whirl until blended. With the motor running, drizzle in the oil in a slow steady stream until thick.